ISBN: 9798837199318

PANDEMIC POETS

An Anthology

Table of Contents

Introduction

Welcome to this anthology of poetry about the COVID-19 (Coronavirus) pandemic. It has been put together over social media, which in itself tells of the forced solitude and restricted opportunities to interact in person; but also that ways can be found to make things happen if we work with the tools available to us, and add a dollop of imagination.

Naturally (or perhaps unnaturally), the pandemic affected every angle and corner of our lives, from the lockdowns and restrictions of movement and sociability, to the financial squeezes of domestic and commercial functionality. There were more negative impacts than positives, but I am told that investments in the pharmaceutical sector performed excellently. Conversely the mental health of humanity was acutely tested and battered, and the effects of that will doubtless be observed long into the future.

Civilisation shifted from initial panic to manufactured and micromanaged hope, driven by hype, to the marshalled propaganda push to place faith in brand new vaccines. Those vaccines were administered around the world prior to full authorisation - though that aspect was not widely shared with the eager participants in the rollouts. The push was assisted and amplified by daily televised coverage on the world-famously impartial BBC, at prime-time, by the Prime Minister, flanked by selected medical boffins with bafflingly lofty-sounding titles. We hadn't seen so many graphs and statistics since school.

It came to permeate every nook and cranny of popular culture, helped by printed and broadcast media doing what they always aim to do........control and manipulate narratives, and in turn the perceptions of the public. They seem to forget that it's the public's money that enables them to exist at all, and surely if there were to be a 'revolution' it would be the public withdrawing their funding to cause

7

the whole sector to implode and disappear - silent and peaceful yet devastating. Imagine the absolute bliss of the aftermath.

What ensued? Some people were obedient. Some were frightened. Others were angry. Everybody, bar none, had a reaction of one kind or another.

Writers that work for, and serve, the media machines, wrote what they were told and allowed to, in delivering their column inches and word counts for their salaries and fees. (They just do jobs at the end of the day, like librarians, chambermaids and telesales reps). There were applecarts to avoid upsetting and masters and paymasters likewise. Certain themes were permitted while certain others were strictly forbidden. And so, to the 'Pandemic Poets'.

This book reflects a whole spectrum of responses, from obedience to fright to anger, and every nuance in between. A sprinkling of forensic analysis too, from pens mightier than swords, as it should have been from the beginning in our and every cuntry (oops, spelling, sorry) where free speech and democracy are sacrosanct. At least that's what our transparent, honest media tell us is the case.

In recent years, the internet, and social media platforms particularly, have been a valuable means of sharing content and information. To share material in this sphere is as easy as pie in a free, liberated culture, but in this case it all became cloaked in censorship and 'fact checkers', that closed like opaque curtains on any and all content that dared to criticise, condemn and complain about the Orwellian controls, and the shadowy corporations allegedly pulling the strings of the interventions. Allegedly.

Poets are compelled to communicate and express themselves. It's not a choice or a conscious decision, but a reflex, an instinctive reaction. Coded into their DNA, you might topically allude.

Automatic. Biological. Compulsive. Driven. Essential.

The words written on these pages might as well have appeared on the paper all by themselves, like blood pouring from opened veins or spraying from opened arteries. They exist because they have to. They come through from the ether, defying mortal attempts to block their way.

Thank you to every poet, both published and unpublished, that has given their time, ability and energy to these pieces of work. The collection is colourful, powerful, unique and culturally important. The variations of style and substance in the Pandemic Poets anthology make for a fascinating and educational adventure.

The poems were written at different stages of the unfolding story, and have not been sorted chronologically, therefore the viewpoints bounce around in both time and space. Our poets hail from many parts of the world. Purists may also notice linguistic inconsistencies, but these are intentional, since poets retain the artistic autonomy (in my opinion) to toy with grammar, syntax and punctuation, and even spelling, if done intentionally and with aplomb.

Stuart Watkins
Curator, Pandemic Poets, July 2022.

Meet the Poets

Jane Badrock

Jane's career, for many a year, was in Finance, until she called time. She painted, she read, now writes fiction instead, and sometimes, ridiculous rhyme.

Hahona Batt

Hahona is from New Zealand. He is a happily married, retired grandfather. Poetry is his passion and refuge, enabling escape from a world seemingly hell bent on conformity.

Briony Bax

Briony is an editor, poet, and social activist. From 2013 - 2020 she edited Ambit Magazine and in 2020 her pamphlet *Lament* was published by Rough Trade Press.
http://www.brionybax.com

Andy Cash

Andy is from Stockport, and influenced by American and British post-war poetry, from Bukowski to Hughes and Heaney, utilising half-rhymes and raw descriptions. His poems have been featured on BBC Radio and in various anthologies.

Lisa Goodwin

Lisa is an Elder Bard of Ynys Witrin (Glastonbury). She won Glastonbury Festival Poetry Slam in 2019, holding the title of Slam champion for three years due to the pandemic.

Isobel Hannah

Isobel is aged 20, from Yorkshire, she has been writing songs and poetry since childhood. She is passionate about LGBTQIA+/human rights. Her in-progress debut novel is a sapphic love story.

Wasim Ul Haque

Wasim is from India, a diverse secular contingent. He loves satire as much as he loves "to spill the beans". That amuses him as much as comedy and drama.

Danielle Haslehurst

Danielle is a published writer from Manchester. She hoards books like dragons hoard gold. She lives with her husband in central Manchester (and her books).

Steve Heyes

Steve is a 73-year-old, living in Chester. Having done an online poetry course, he started writing seriously during the pandemic, incensed by the actions of politicians and the population.

Tina Keophannga

Tina is an artist and writer from the USA, and her inspirations come from that direct experience and everyday life.

Anne Korhonen

Anne, also known as Eyeslikeblues, is a Finnish copywriter, poet and spoken word artist. Her sophomore poetry book Poems of Universal Love is available from Amazon.

Sharon Larkin

Sharon has a pamphlet, *Interned at the Food Factory* (Indigo Dreams, 2019) and a collection, *Dualities* (Hedgehog Poetry Press, 2020) … and over 200 poems in anthologies, magazines, and e-zines.

Sarah Laurel

Sarah is an artist/designer from Yorkshire, UK. Sarah painted the back cover during lockdown, then the front in 2022 to create the full book cover design.

Terri Lee-Shield

Terri is a designer, artist and activist from the Northeast of England. Fascinated by life and an advocate for nature, she writes poetry as a form of personal expression.

Peter W Levi

Peter William Levi is a wordsmith that hammers out Concrete Poetry, a form of poetry that focuses on the aesthetics. He's known for his profound views and his complex rhyming.

Anna Maria Mickiewicz

Anna Maria Mickiewicz lives in London. Founder of the publishing house Literary Waves. Her poetic works have appeared in the United States, UK, Australia, Canada, Poland, Mexico, Italy, Bulgaria, Hungary, Salvador and India.

Boomie Miles

Boomie is a poet and author from Toledo, Ohio. He writes layered perspectives about his views on life, resulting in heart/thought provoking pieces. Author of W.O.W - Waves of War (2021).

Kathryn O'Driscoll

Kathryn is a UK slam champion and World Slam finalist (2021), a poet and activist from Bath. She talks openly about disabilities, mental health, LGBTQIA+ issues, and survival in her poems.

Charlene Phare

Charlene is married with 2 children and has grandchildren; she lives in England. She says the world is her inspiration, there's a poem right there!

Serpens Ptolemy

Serpens is a professor of mathematics, intellectual snob, and dabbler in the writing of poetry. He is not an Egyptian snake, or an Egyptian, or a snake.

Sunil Sharma

Dr. Sunil Sharma, ophthalmologist, writes poems and articles in Hindi and English, regularly published in local newspapers and monthlies. He has had two Hindi poetry collections and five joint collections published.

Lee Smith

This 62-year-old, singing AI man turned to poetry seven years ago, publishing last year. He writes of events and life experiences through rhyming couplets.

Christine Smuniewski

Christine is a 29-year-old poet in Tennessee, United States. Poetry gets her through both her best and darkest days. Her dachshund is the centre of her world.

Gae Stenson

Gae, a late bloomer, gained an English degree at 38 and a Creative Writing MA at 57. Currently, she is working on her first novel, focussing on society's outsiders.

Rose Stevens

Rose writes poetry on Instagram as Rosa Poet, @poetrosapoetry and has been chronicling the politics of the pandemic. She also writes short stories and has just finished a novel.

Hannah Stone

Hannah has published several collections of poetry and collaborates with other poets and composers. She is poet-theologian for Leeds Church Institute, edits Dream Catcher journal and facilitates literary gatherings in Leeds.

Janet Tai

Janet is a 61-year-old Malaysian-Chinese poet. She is a retiree and one of her favourite pastimes is writing poems in her free verse style.

Stuart Watkins

Stuart has authored three ground-breaking books:
'A United Kingdom' - Trains of Logical Thought (2019)
Cosmic Visions (2021)
The Ocean (2021)
Available from Amazon.
He loves collaborating with musicians.

Georgina Wilding

Georgina is the former Creative Director of Nottingham Poetry Festival and the 2017- 2019 Nottingham Young Poet Laureate. Her debut poetry collection, Hag Stone, is out now with Verve Poetry Press.

Stuart Williamson

Stuart, a sculptor by profession, is a native of coastal Yorkshire, but now lives in Ecuador with his wife Mary, and their two sons.

Whispering Trees

Isobel Hannah

Do the trees hear your whispers?
I break away from life
to wander woods with worried eyes.
Lies of borrowing time,
work life strife balances on thin lines.

I used to be able to create.
Paint feminine figures
or play the melodies of myth and infatuation.

It's shaken from my mind
by the mass administration of corporations.

Do I really need a standard education?
Blatant lack of diversifying the curriculum and nation
Have patience to travel,
a system of borders
permitting freedom of location

Skin crawls like an infestation
at the sight of children dying
Prying open the door of blissful Western ignorance
Sins of bombs dropped on schools,
ignored by privileged indifference

Is this how we experience our world?
Observed from ivory towers,
power to the one per cent

A perfect descent
into dystopian hierarchical torment

I want to break the systemic cycle
A Bible of know your place,
wars against embrace.
Fundamentally we are flawed
but power comes from our grace

Do you feel the energy of the breeze?
Please understand
it is the same air we all breathe.
A message of peace
seems futile coming from clenched teeth.

So, relax your jaw,
breathe in deep

Perceive the world
with the innocence
of whispering trees.

Herd Mentality

Sharon Larkin

What panicked the sheep was invisible.

One second, ewes were grazing in green pastures,

the next, a report from some silent starting pistol

sent them sprinting, faster than ovines

should ever have reason to travel.

Nothing pursued them -

no hound or horse or bird of prey.

No farmer had come to tempt his girls

with trailer-loads of beets or hay

but some were leaping lamb-like,

all hooves aloft, then turning, as one,

to charge again from whence they came,

stampeding forth and back beside the wall

which some began to clamber on,

to disappear beyond - where a year before,

we found a sheep's corpse, bones picked clean.

We knew a steep slope fell away

a few feet further on, into the quarry below,

feared a lemming-like scene there,

wondered what weed or bane, opioid or hemp,

could drive beasts to madness such as this.

Back home, we're alarmed by news

of stock market crashes, supermarket dashes,

clashes in aisles as folk go overboard

for toilet rolls.

We can't make sense of theories

about herd immunity

or appeals for distance and isolation

as sixty thousand flock for four days on the trot

to the races, and others jump

aboard their last flight home.

(Previously published at Atrium, 10 April 2020)

Green Hour

Georgina Wilding

Something so small as an hour
has arrived on my doorstep. As it happens,
each of us has one to choose from.
Some of them smell of flasked coffee
in dawn hands. Others, like the bitter evidence
of a bike ride in the short shadows of evening.
All of them take us somewhere green -
to the lawns where Pansy's black mouths open oh',
the square recreations of cut grass and goal posts,
or memorial sites of wreath and stone.
We wonder what we'd look to without parks,
what they might be after all this worship.
Like us, the green's had time to stop
and consider itself.

A COVID Ode

Stuart Watkins

I'm off to Newcastle, to purchase some coal,

I'm digging my garden, to make a deep, dark hole.

I'm scared of that Omicron on the BBC,

and the Alpha and the Delta on the ITV.

'Government briefings', of relentless hype.

Tabloid announcements, in front page type.

Quaxxine commercials, like laser beams.

YouTube deletions, by 'Fact Check' teams.

COVID mutates every time we blink,

and it needs much more than the kitchen sink;

we must have a jab every time that we're told,

as it seems so much worse than a Common Cold

or a bout of Flu, a splutter or sneeze,

it's the Big Pandemic, a deadly disease.

If I don't act fast, and ask "how high?"

when ordered to jump, I'm going to die.

My natural immunity won't be enough.

Even if my constitution's tough.

I need more jabs! So does my child!

This terrible virus is scampering wild!

Don't listen to those that don't believe!

It's not an opinion, like 'Remain' v 'Leave'!

The media gave us our Brexit wet dream!

Pharmaceutical shares are the Fat Cats' cream.

They kept it 'schtum', the 'emergency use',

or the vaccine drive might have looked like abuse.

It's 'The Science', therefore it cannot be wrong,

"I did my research" so my knowledge is strong;

a 'Conspiracy Theorist' if I disagree,

(a term designed to discredit me).

23

Where's that Professor's lecture I share
on my Facebook page? It isn't there.

It's disappeared, I can't post for a week,
I inherit the Earth, but am unable to speak,
on social media I'm rendered the meek,
insignificant, cancelled, fragile and weak.

It's a Propaganda War, make no mistake,
but see the Ivory Towers start to crumble and quake.

The secrets are out. The lies are exposed.
The BBC suits are all calm and composed.
They tell us the truth (but only a portion)
they try to pretend that there's no dark distortion.
Nothing is hidden. Nothing withheld.

Transparent.

The Truth.
Trustworthy.

SELLED.

(......."Sold" doesn't rhyme. Dammit. You get it.)

(You get it whether you want it or not.)

**(From the upcoming poetry collection
'Cataclysmic Vibrations')**

All the Poets United

Andy Cash

Another lockdown, but not in the mind
As we scramble to desks, pens, and arms
To fight against you, take the viral demon down
In veins, hearts, deep into the lacquered lungs

From the dirt in the air, the filth some smoked
The food binged, bodies abused, but survived
Dreams removed by the market efficiency
But the Poets Unite in the darkest living hours

The words, their worlds collide, composites
Brilliantly crafted to take back what is ours
Freedom valued, and now traded for longer lives
In this Town, within a Town, and its Hall of Halls

These thoughts, the beacon of the beautiful
The flowering in tournamented text voiced
Our own people, the creation of the community
From coffeehouses, masked choirs to church wards

The script is written again, in the same year
My fellowship flies, soaring above, to take aim
Braving the mental illness of mankind's death
A few, and the viral fever cannot win this war

She talks, to the screen of the windows, into life
Dorinda is framed in her own downstairs room
With family free to play a backgrounded bit part
Her pen of courage is mighty for Stockport Town

Her life everlasting, pitched in memories
The marvellous mindfulness of her soft voice
Lifts those words of wisdom from the page
And all is bright, in the second Lockdown wave

Pandemic Nightmare

Steve Heyes

The boggart that is COVID has mutated into a new strain

Strain on people's faces as it is devoted to causing deaths

Deaths exacerbated by people not adhering to rules

Rules to stay indoors and protect the hospitals

Hospitals buckling under the weight of patients

Patients admitted as others thought they were above rules

Rules ignored by attending illegal parties breaking the law

Law breakers upset when they get fined as dummies

Dummies' ignorance as mobs of COVID deniers protest

Protest maskless ignoring social distancing

Distancing from the facts shouting abuse at nurses

Nurses witnessing COVID's deathly toll

Tolls decline as lockdowns continue to slowly work

Work continues but some still ignore limitations

Limitations of their intellect which must be defective

Defective moral compass with no foundations

The March of COVID Frontline Soldiers

Sunil Sharma

We march
we the health workers
and volunteers
to save humanity
without any equipment
ventilators or even oxygen
without any drugs either
with no kits
the vaccines too disappear
with our hands tied back
still we march

We march
we the reporters
to save humanity
we report
the ugly administration
we expose the hoarders
of drugs and essentials

We the COVID frontline soldiers….
We march
we march
to save humanity

Thoughts From the Jetty

Janet Tai

Here I sit…,
By the jetty
Watching…,
Fishing boats
Come and go
At the close…
Of a frenzied evening;

Here I sit…
By the jetty
Legs in…
Ankle-deep waters
Admiring the sunset
Taking in…
The warm fishy air;

Here I sit…,
Alone
Pondering…
In this…
Meditative loneliness;

About life…
As 61 approaches
About the…,
Remains of my days;

Wondering…
About…
The uncertainties
Of this
Pandemic stricken
World;

Wondering…
How to…
Lend my words…
To echo…
The fate
Of the suffering
And the
Downtrodden!!!

The Silent Beast

Stuart Williamson

The silent beast stalks
In our breath, in the air
It's there on our hands,
On our lips, in our hair
And we are its prey
And we hide in our rooms
If we 're tempted to wander
We go to our doom

It favours the poor
And the aged, poor souls
And cares not a bit
For the plans we unfold
And the rich politicians
Crank up their machines
In some desperate attempt
To go back as things were…

But there are no, 'things were'
They're all gone, and won't be
The same anymore
And neither will we
And they don't give a damn
For the workers, it's cruel
They sit in their suits
Those Panjandrumic fools

They're the people we voted for

They haven't a clue
And they don't really care
If it's me or it's you
That goes down with this bug
They're still in their seats
And they'll ride it all out
With their coffers replete

It's all very quiet
Out there on the streets
Just a few crazy bastards
Imagining they're free
Waving machine guns
And carrying their signs
They are the Pro-Death folks
With desperate designs

Animals are wandering
In the emptied-out streets
And the birds fill the blue skies
It's almost a treat
Does it mean there's a chance
To start fresh and reach out?
For a much better world
Than the one we're without

PMQ's

Lee Smith

Can the Prime Minister confirm there was a party?
To the honourable member I say no
Then he has misled Parliament
And to the tower he must go
It was a work event
That the honourable member seeks to define
And his request for me to go
I respectfully decline
I have no recollection of a gathering unlawful
And find the implication nothing short of awful
I was in my residence
And oft partake of wine
And therefore see no reason that I should face a fine.

Coronavirus Shopping Time

Anna Maria Mickiewicz

Pirouettes with the baskets
Coronavirus dance in a supermarket

Gloves are ready
For the ballet

Masks on the faces
Time for a carnival,
Time for Venice

Recipe for Disorder

Lisa Goodwin

I found this recipe in an old Zion cookbook, written
some time past when the world was really crook.
Translated by a keyworker, now discredited. An eX
weatherman and viraloadologist.

Before you start, prepare the space and wear a
white hat wrapped in foil, just in case. Get a soapy
bowl of political disillusionment, and liberally wash
all of your ingredients.

Gaslight oven to 666 and fluff up concern with a
high-tech risk.

Take some science and fiction, in equal measure,
mix in dubious news at your leisure. Then get some
research, finely grated, with a pinch of fake truth,
copied and pasted. Heavily marinate until over-inflated.
Set aside a few hours, add some drama and taste it.

After you have completed this stage, Microsoftly
knead some rage. In a Petri dish of COVID morbidity,
to breakdown knowledge and soften rigidity.

Incorporate some dissonance into the fold, with a
YouTube feed full of tired out tropes. Build up
momentum until the plot thickens, then over-egg
liberally with complaints of Nazism. Reach a high

temperature, invoke Godwin's law, and cover it with
a pocket full of panic porn.

Press together heavily with a splash of CAPS LOCK DOWN!
Bring it all together with a CONTAGION OF THE CROWN!
Next, you'll have to manifest a SECRET ingredient,
to capitalise on consistent obedience.
Consider a green tablet instead of red or blue,
stir with a Matrix spoon.

Lastly, take a cup of 5G essence, and if that's not
available use common nonsense. Whip it up into a
soft topped peak, use a pan or a plan and Wi-Fri lightly.

This may make a sticky mess of the area, but you
can clean up later with anti-fact dysphoria.

Half-baked at home for over 6 weeks, before taking
it out and spiking it with WikiLeaks. While it's still
warm, if you really must, add adrenogoogle drizzle
and then dust, with nano chemtrail particle space
age Musk.

When your conspirituality is finally completed, it's
time to sit down, you can't have your cake and eat it.
Serve up iced, with a glass of passive aggression,
but please watch out for cognitive indigestion.

That Spring

Hannah Stone

That was the spring you could walk down the middle
of the road, stone cold sober, at 2pm, and no-one
batted an eyelid. After a week of awkward elbow-
bumps we settled for eyeing each other suspiciously
above over-worked smiles. We texted exes with offers
of support, and the moral high ground made molehills
out of mountains. And you remembered that moles
are blamed for tunnelling listeria under pasture-land,
and that badgers are blamed for bovine TB, and rats
vilified for the Black Death when it was in fact the
parasites that caused it, the fleas that swelled with
pride at their power. And you recalled John Donne's
poem about the flea, the only metaphysical poet to
make insect bites sexy as fuck. And that was the
spring the leader of the free world called this the
Chinese virus and said that he was looking forward to
churches full of worshippers next Sunday, and the
spring when some of us believed his delusional
arrogance was the biggest contagious risk
imaginable. And the spring when you mused that
social distancing might result in a new chastity, and at
the same time how lockdown would bring a spike in
the birth-rate come Christmas. And the sky was so
blue and the sun so warm it was hard to believe there
would be a Good Friday before the Resurrection and,
coming back to the rats for a minute, you caught the
latest news bulletin and heard that Parliament was

closing now, until after the Easter Recess. And each
day you woke and heard birdsong in place of rush
hour traffic you opened your lungs to the world and
the air was like champagne

There Were No Parties

Rose Stevens

You took the piss
You had a laugh
We're just like your cleaning staff
and your security guards
following rules and working hard
and getting insults and abuse
if we dare to say the use
of Number 10 as a wine bar
was pushing COVID rules too far
While you told us what to do
at press conferences, you knew
that afterwards you'd drink some wine
with colleagues - you say it's fine
though we weren't allowed to bend
the rules to visit sick friends
or say goodbye at funerals
We'd be branded criminals
But you let staffers get away
with regular Wine Time Fridays
let them party through the night
(some of them got in a fight)
order pizza and drink fizz
throw up, and have a quiz
Often you would rock up too
we've seen photos showing you
standing next to booze-filled tables
yet, somehow, it seems you're able
to tell us that at all times

rules were followed. Bare-faced lies
Sue said there was no respect
for cleaners and guards, both subject
to 'poor treatment' from your team
I can't help thinking there's a theme
that seems to be emerging here
your sneering defence makes it clear
that if we dare to complain
we'll get contempt and disdain
We must get it in our heads
you're the boss and we're the plebs

COVID Nation

Peter W Levi

All these people trapped in homes,
Constantly scrolling through phones,
With so much family time to spend,
But we'll just complain in the end,
Unable to count these blessings,
Or learning from older lessons,
It's time to be moving forwards,
With your dreams and more words.

More COVID nation.
It's our salvation,
We thank creation,
For COVID nation.
Cause this sensation,
Is like translation
From COVID nation.

Now we have time for us,
Or we'll make a big fuss,
Future now in our hands,
Our destiny we command,
Maybe try something new,
Bravely even without a clue,
Have fun and find passion,
And no more self-bashing.

More COVID nation,
It's our salvation,

We thank creation,

For COVID nation.
Cause this sensation,
Is like translation
From COVID nation.

Every blessing has its curse,
We're in heaven but it's worse,
Some will not make it though,
But in this hard life what's new,
We must die so we can ascend,
And there is no way to pretend,
But who we lose God will gain,
So please don't feel any strain.

More COVID nation,
It's our salvation,
We thank creation,
For COVID nation.
Cause this sensation,
Is like translation,
From COVID nation.

The Sound of Human Kindness

Briony Bax

This town sits nestled on the North Norfolk Coast.
Its quay bristling with lobster pots.
See plastic catch trays stacked along the sea wall,
The fishing fleet, salt marsh beyond,
The endless beach, wind farm harbour,
and generations of lifeboat crew.

A town with butchers and bakers,
Well used pubs and tea-rooms,
fish and chip takeaways with a '99 flake,
ancient walkways used by smugglers,
higgledy houses with priest holes and
brightly painted beach huts, legs buried in sand.

COVID-19 struck Norfolk early that Spring.
Doors were locked, public meetings cancelled.
Only essential shops stayed open.
Fear tore down Two Furlong Hill, up Burnt Lane
Through Jolly Sailor Yard
And whistled around Northfields.

Wells became a ghost town.
Gone were the tourists, the crabbers,
The day trippers and the beach combers.

Furtive shoppers and quietly between
Howells, Nisa and Jaggers. Shopped quickly,
Anxious to get back to the safety of their homes.

Outsiders were banished.
Police received complaints from suspicious neighbours.
They knocked on doors, sent rule-breakers home.
Masks were worn, the two-metre rule enforced.
Church communion was suspended.
Kissing, hugging and singing, all were banned.

But while the town was in the silent fog of fear,
Skeins of hope wound through the streets.
Like shafts of sun on sea after a storm.
People looked outward and offered their help.
Children of essential workers went back to school.
The Carnival Committee entertained online.

A schoolgirl wrote poems for nurse's funds.
Flowers decked graves for absent loved ones.
Lifeboat teams volunteered at vaccine clinics.
Roasts were delivered to NHS workers.
The theatre streamed at-home offerings.
The god of Zoom became the saviour of connection.
The self-isolating and shielding were supported.
A widow found friends she hadn't known.
A gluten free loaf was baked for a paramedic.
Small and personal tasks would be completed unasked,
Not for fanfare, money or fame,
But the simple goodness of the thing.
A new heart was heard beating,

In the clinking of masts on a quiet creek.
The tap, tap, tap, of East wind at keyholes.
Footsteps on cobbles, a sea shanty beat,
Sweeter than a high tide in summer.
Human kindness reverberated throughout the town.

**(Commissioned by the 'Wells of Human Kindness'
exhibit in Wells-next-the-Sea)**

The Scaremonger

Serpens Ptolemy

Hey! You!

What'll we do?

Give me a jab

or I'll be on a slab.

How to escape

the 'needle rape'?

Where to hide?

Do I stay inside?

Telly is full

of vaccine bull.

The Press as one

blocks the sun.

I can't sleep

but daren't peep.

My locked house,

quiet as a mouse.

Can't go out.

There's Death about.

Reaping souls.

Burning coals.

Where's the end?

Around the bend?

Or is there none?

Unblock the sun!

Noli Me Tangere

Sharon Larkin

We avoid alley, ginnell, snicket, jigger,

favour wider lanes in rural areas

for dubious doses of fresh air, sun.

Handshakes, hugs are supplanted

first by elbow bumps, then clasping

our own hands across our chests,

gestures of intent, no eye contact.

A raised palm declares touch me not.

A nod while staring at our own feet.

Perfume from that girl trails

behind for yards, sneaks sideways

up nostrils, stirs unease, disgust.

Late night treks to supermarkets,

scarf bandit-like around mouth

and nose. Gloves, strict time limits,

bills kept below the swipe amount,

breath held at checkouts, gasping

to the door as if already a case.

Fingers wagging through glass:

Leave it on the step, sign for me.

Spraying deliveries and doorknobs.

Neural networks retrained

to ban fingers from facial orifices,

handwashing to Happy Birthday,

Jerusalem, God Save the Queen

or Killing in the name of. Asking

will these hands ever be clean?

**(Previously published in New Boots and Pantisocracies,
Postcards from Malthusia, 9 April 2020)**

Heat

Danielle Haslehurst

Throat caressed by fire
Unstressed and undressed
Bed-bound by lethargy, not desire,
The room gets hot
The room, mind, I'm not,
I'm coping, I'm fine, just a cough
Let's not kick off unrestrained distress
Just remain unstressed
And remedy undressed with a layer
Then another
Place one on top of the other
Add blankets and shiver
Feel faint and deliver at the first hint of dread
Bed-bound in bed
With the room getting hotter
And has the fever now got her?
Not sure if I'm she but I'd rather be
Unstressed and undressed but I'm layered in layers
The water's run dry and I've no hydration to cry
I pile on the layers and I shiver
I wonder why I'm getting colder and colder
The fever is bolder
I resign to call out, my body in drought,
The fever-dream wait as I fever-see my fate
More layers and layers
Then - answer to my prayers!
My husband returns
He has run back from work

Now he must run to work
To remove my layers, to quench the drought
The doctor advises my condition is in doubt
Asthma, you say?
The hospital on the horizon
But no, just cool her, you're doing a good job, my son
Just cool and hydrate
The fever will abate
Leave her unstressed and undressed
Monitor, stay by her,
With throat caressed by fire.

Heavenly Trip

Lee Smith

It started with a cough
And then a little sneeze
And very quickly afterwards
I felt I couldn't breathe
They took me in an ambulance
In the middle of the night
They placed a mask upon my face
I felt I should surely die
A host of angels then I saw
Believed I was at death's door
Masked faces dressed in green or blue
They said we'll do our best for you
They catered for my every need
Fought to reverse my destiny
May the Lord forever bless
The workers of the NHS

Escapism

Charlene Phare

Chucky chains jingle, still struggling
Padlocked firmly into place
Certainly juggling
Sealed steel box, suspended up high
Flames licking, teasing it
Wishing to fly
Race has begun, timers are set
Heart beating fast, loudly
Forget regret
Contortionist, scrunched up tightly
Scrabbling for keys. clanging
Desperate plea
Play music loud, over again
Discover adventures
Dance in the rain
Metal chinked as it hit the floor
Suddenly releasing
Freedom once more

The New World

Terri Lee-Shield

A new world is being created and sweeping across the land
and never again will we witness being underhand.
It is not for anyone to force their will on any other,
If we truly cared, we would respect each and the other.

Work together for peace and protect what you hold dear
by loving them well and keeping your intention clear.
For weakness is bred when we meddle in another
and strength through arms is abusing your brother.

The virus is here, it is not going away,
We cannot control it as part of creation it stays.
It's not for people to delve into things they don't understand,
our only duty is to be ourselves and care for this land.

For God gave us choice and fate gave us free will,
we punish ourselves when we torture and kill.
Do what you need, what you know to be right
Do not force another, cause violence and fight.

Mercy is found in allowing all who are living
to be as they feel and contribute through giving.
For none can control who lives and who dies

but we can stop spreading fear, confusion and lies.

It is not for you to give away all of your power
but bloom in uniqueness like each wonderful flower.
Because all is needed if we want to survive
Non-violence essential if we want to thrive.

There is no answer to this sorry tale
but follow your guidance and leave others to fail.
For God is our body, our mind and our heart
Fate is what is left once all is done and we depart.

These words have been written for those that need to hear it,
life is going to kill you but there is no reason to fear it.
Those who can live with love and peace in their heart
always take it with us when we depart.

People cannot live in ways that harm the Earth
Nature will not abide us ruining her worth.
Life is not about toiling, struggle and pain,
Nor is it about only your material gain.

Life is to life in its fullest expression,
in the way we see fit and not through succession.
Living through the spirit we feel deep inside
and giving love freely with nurture and pride.

The time has come where all have both kinds,
God's strength and protection and Fate's feeling and mind.

We need to consider the implications
and what it really means
to take away a person's spirit
and crush their hopes and dreams.
The new world is here and we all play a part
by letting go of fear and and living through your heart.
Each has been blessed with their own way, view and song,
and none are all right and nothing is wrong.

You'll know this message is true as you feel it in your body,
let it take away your fears, your anger, any source of worry,
Fate is now in motion and there is little you can do,
use your lifetime wisely, spend it being you!

The Visibility of the Toxicity

Stuart Watkins

It's the Agenda.

The Propaganda.

Rammed down our throats,

from Land's End to John O'Groats.

The year is Twenty Twenty Two,

the Ownership of Me and You.

Our Freedom, Eroded,

our Reality, Decoded,

our Nerves, Corroded

by Explosives, Exploded.

The Media Manipulation

and Messaging Mutation,

this Viral Velocity,

this COVID Conspiracy,

controlled Communications,

Cancerous Collaborations,

the Agenda,

the Propaganda.

Orwell foresaw it,

'Nineteen Eighty-Four-d' it.

Huxley foretold it,

like the Walls of Colditz.

Prisons made of Words,

Immunities of Herds,

Diseases that we Breathe

through the Webs our Spiders Weave;

the World Wide Needles jab

like the Pincers of a Crab,

which pierce our feeble skin

to inject their wares within.

Thoughts bent like Metals,

using Vices and Vessels

and Darkness and Light,

by Day and by Night,

each sense is a Courier,

a Deliverer, a Poisoner.

Perpetual Motion

Divides our Devotion.

Devilish Distractions,

Fatal Attractions.

Stimuli Stretched,

like Eternity Etched

on the Minds and the Hearts

and the Maps and the Charts.

Our Paths and our Vew.

Our Compass is True.

Malleable Men,

Masked brethren,

Whispers in Ears

draw Laughter and Tears.

Control is the Aim,

the Psyche the Frame,

the Agenda.

The Propaganda.

Those Grips made of Lies

are Imaginary ties.

Autonomy's Intact

if the Software is hacked.

Retention of belief;

your Soul is your Chief.

As you tuned yourself in,

you may tune out again.

Take hold of your truth,

climb onto the roof,

look around and about,

see the Sky through the doubt.

These Houses of Cards

are in a Typhoon of Rage,

bars made from your Own Will

are forming that Cage.

Surrendering your Power

is an Optional Act;

It's not a Matter of Opinion,

It's a Matter of Fact.

**(From the forthcoming poetry collection
'Cataclysmic Vibrations')**

Another Day, Another Mask

Christine Smuniewski

They said last year this would be over
but some knew better than that.
These various trials are a
part of this thing we call life.
The tragedies, the authoritative trajectories -
it's all included in this inclusive section of our existence.
Some believed a vaccine would fix it.
A mask - minimise its potential.
We remember the donations for ventilators
and how the world came together just like in times past.
Thankful - that it wasn't times past and
praying our exposure to its layers will die down fast
like a Zamboni on an ice-skating rink
which comes to clean up the mess.

The Pandemic Special

Kathryn O'Driscoll

Hi there!
Oh, you're here for the pandemic?

Baking sourdough, loo roll shortage, Peleton, Hamilton, BoJo
bollocks, health care cock ups, clap for your carers, murder hornets,
Joe Wicks' workouts, Duolingo owl; Can you say Systemic Racism?
choosing between protesting for your human rights
and your safety, global PTSD,
Twitter news, daily briefings, zoom meetings
(coulda been an email),
hand sanitizer, retrained in cyber, display bookcases, banana bread,
Animal Crossing, Dominic Cummings,
should have gone to Specsavers,
Captain Tom marching on, buying sweatpants, Bridgerton,
Tiger King, that bitch Carole Baskin, Nightingale hospitals,
working from home,
got a new puppy, got a new hobby, making masks, food parcels,
got time for a skin care routine, a long-distance love affair,
bin bags as protective gear, a chance to polish up your CV,
joining TikTok ironically - *soon may the Wellerman come* -
singing lessons remotely,
5am addiction, queer awakening, folklore, evermore, homemade
mullet, the Masked Singer, baby Yoda,
singing happy birthday to yourself on your birthday,
and every day
and every other day,
boredom.
A pandemic full of
nothing.

I'm so sorry we don't actually have any more of those
available right now…

We only have the disabled persons' option on the menu.
But it comes with a whole foray of new features!

16 months locked inside, people saying they'd rather let you just die,
access suddenly being taken seriously
when it affects everybody,
choosing between reaching out for help
when you're struggling and your safety,
social media specialists available 24/7
to tell you you're imagining it,
discharged with COVID into care homes without quarantine,
letters telling you that you should be shielding
after the first lockdown has ended,
can't see your support network,
no carers in hospital appointments,
no grocery delivery slots,
18 month waiting lists,
access being revoked,
shielding ended, still no vaccine,
free online will services,
discussing your funeral with your fiancé,
elderly, disabled, learning difficulties,
autistic, neurodivergent.

Do not resuscitate orders
signed by your doctors
without your permission.

Do not resuscitate orders
signed by doctors
without permission.
900 of us dead with DNRs that we did not sign.

Do not resuscitate orders signed by our doctors
without our
permission.

60% of deaths despite being only 18% of the population,
exhausted by the enormity of grief, can't catch my breath,
can't catch a break,
government whiteboard says
"who do we not save?"

Me.

They don't want to save me.

So, I'll sign you up for our eugenics special sweetie.
No, I'm sorry. It's not optional. But have a super 2020.

Global Warning Agendas

Boomie Miles

Clone me, own me, chip me, flip me, brain electricity,
AI controlling, truth seeking and exposing before they try to silence me
out, label me crazy, all these surgeries with tubes in their mouth,
knocked out, melanin and carbon carved out.

They mentioned 5G more likely it's a 10G, billionaires taking
vacations to space, Congress won't even stimulate me.
Nano technology, programs being made like games, DNA strands
changed, body alterations, celebrities snaking the future generations,
vaccine metals making us machines and slaves, agendas cancelling
the straight, while the gays run the stage, RFID chips getting placed
with no trace, they make us focus on race, while power lines
monopolised frequencies putting modes in our minds, no matter white
or black lives, culture vultures setting trends to distract us with lies.

All these Babies missing, they're tryna block out the sun, elites want to
be God, ungodlike, they wanna keep us at home, adrenachrome,
pychops, cryptocurrency, more new variants. New world order, molech
owls, cloud seeding, global governance. Mark of the Beast, chemtrails
and dry wells, MK Ultra, jezebel spirits lurking,
eyes I try to open.

Stay prayed up 2020 was the wake-up Satan tryna place us in the lake
but my God is so much greater. Tracking Surveillances, big brothers
watching wicked doctrines spreading amongst the masses, Corona
spreading even faster? Delta pyramid mathematics, what I say?
Vaccine you can keep far away self-care n I pray our faith in the Lord
will give us grace for these wicked and strange days.

Global Warning theory!?!

Ode to COVID

Jane Badrock

When
2019 came
and   went,
We were in
quite good cheer.
'Twas better than
the year before,
if not the greatest year.
With 2020 came the hope
That things might work out right.
With perfect vision, things resolved
Less rainy and days more bright.
But COVID-19 tracked us down, it rained and things got wetter.
And when the sun came out it was too late to make things better.
We had a lockdown, thousands died, the NHS was breaking
Our care homes couldn't take the strain, hearts and minds were aching.
Things started to improve a bit - but cracks began appearing
More tiers and tears are on the news we're all so tired of hearing.
With Christmas soon upon us now. we yearn for health and healing.
We want to look for better times We're fed up with this feeling.
So 2020 listen up.
You came here
By a cough.
The vaccine's
on its way at last,
So will you please FUCK OFF!!!

69

Isolation

Gae Stenson

Still the stars shine
the sun's light
reflects
off the moon
in pools
at your feet
standing sadly
alone
on the beach
waiting
for me.
I
on the other side
of a dying world
stare sadly
at the sky
knowing now
there is no escaping
self-less-isolation.
So,
I stare at the same stars
pretending
I'm where you are
apart
but together
alone
on Skype.

Love in the Time of Corona

Anne Korhonen

Love in the time of corona
The pain of sir and Mona

He cannot stand her face
Look but don't touch is the order
Lipstick sealed letters cross borders
The heart of dreaded disorder
She cannot stand his face
Love lockdown brought the stress at home

Love in the time of corona
The pain of sir and Mona

COVID Haikus

Steve Heyes

COVID vaccine
Rapid rollout in time
Slow virus cases

EU slow action
To vaccinate more
Threatens us all

Socrates Awaiting

Anna Maria Mickiewicz

How to describe the scent of a spring raging with colours
That is impossible.
How many impossibilities are here...
Socrates saddened
Looking at the closed circle of the quarantine

If You Can't Water a Plant Regularly Don't Water It At All

Wasim Ul Haque

One fine Monday,
A young fellow with a big heart
happened to cross the path of a mendicant
in a very unlikely fashion.
He is a man of deeds;
He brought a meal for the day
And embraced him in a friendly attire.

The mendicant was blessed
He pondered if an angel happened to pass by.
For certainly, the world is cruel and dry.

But that's for the day
And like every other day It ends!
And the young fellow went his way.
The next day, the mendicant felt
Utterly disappointed
For the angel didn't appear
He waited for a whole eternity
And yet the angel
Seemed to have forgotten.

The mendicant grew more impatient
And ditched his hitherto endurance
To withstand the cold
For he was given a taste of the warmth.

In the Age of the Pandemic

Stuart Williamson

If I'm unfortunate to find
Too soon the Reaper waiting there
For me to pack my bags
And stamp my card
I hope that I can leave undone
The myriad things
I've left behind, and meant to do
Undecided and forgotten threads
Just when I was on the verge
Or so I thought
Of making sense of what we share
For a little while
All too short it seems
And yet sometimes
We fall apart and can't recall
Or, find our limbs won't make the trek
Better to enjoy the best
Of what we get
And not complain or moan or weep
In fact embrace what best we can
And thank all that, which made it good

High Riders

Sharon Larkin

We were wondering whether we were brave enough
to venture out after three months
of shielded lockdown,
to play cat and mouse with Coronavirus,

while Doug and Bob were on our screen,
pristine in SpaceX white, set to ride the Dragon,
taking risks, orders of magnitude higher
than poking their noses outside their front door.

**(Published in The Pandemic Poetry Anthology,
Gloucestershire Poetry Society, 30 May 2020)**

My Happy Place

Peter W Levi

I'm in my happy place,
Relaxing and rhyming.
I'm in my happy place,
Climaxing the timing.
I'm in my happy place.

I'm all alone,
But not lonely.
I'm in the zone,
Ain't a phony.
Love to write,
Through the day.
About my insight,
Rhyming away.

Counting beats,
Rhythm repeats.
Spinning words,
Reading to birds.
All these true claims,
Playing word games.
And all this for fun,
There now I'm done.
In my happy place,
Relaxing and rhyming.
In my happy place,
Climaxing the timing.
In my happy place.

77

New Year's Eve

Janet Tai

Before….
The pandemic
Restaurants are
Fully booked
Clubs….
Heavily decorated
Alcohol well stocked
Revellers getting ready
To celebrate….
A norm across
The world;

Now
With the pandemic
Still hovering….
Hospital beds
Are fully booked
Mortuaries are….
Overloaded
Modified trailers
Are now….
Makeshift mortuaries
Front liners….
Overworked;

Where?
Where?
Is the joy

The cause
To celebrate?
Is the mood
Ever the same?

For the apathetic
Life goes on….
Alcohol still flows
Revellers still dance
To usher in….
The New Year;

What's….
The significance?
It's just another day
A new….
12-month calendar
A knowledge….
That a new year
Has arrived!!!
'Tis better….
To dial down
And say….
A morning prayer
For the stricken

Momento Monotony

Tina Keophannga

Every day is somehow exactly the same
And different in its own way
It rains
It snows
The sun shines
Pushing daisies
Urgency
An hour
A day
A month
A year
The cold hand of time
Look away
1,000,000
Likely more
Denial
It makes me sad.
And yet
Every day is exactly the same

The Lockdown

Sunil Sharma

The shopping mall was
As busy as a hive
The parkings were bursting
The escalators were zooming
Up and down
The shopping carts were full
And the counters were ringing

Suddenly
Everything stopped
The roads were bare
The industries shut down
The high-rise societies banned
Hawkers and maids
The economy staggered to a halt
The daily wagers had no money

People ran to their roots
The villages, where they were sure
They wouldn't die of hunger
Some walked with their kin
Cops beat them for their fayre
Many fell on the way
Survival was at stake

Such was the terror of virus
But humanity never fails
Samaritans reached desolates

With meals
Arranged transport
Even free rail tickets
To assure them
Return when it dies

The deadly virus!!

COVID Split

Serpens Ptolemy

The ease of it.

The banana split.

Split decision.

Split precision.

Splitting society

with silent sobriety.

Splitting minds,

the snake unwinds.

A proxy war.

The keeping score.

A poisonous bite

of wrong v right,

a painful sting,

an evil thing.

This virus plays

an end of days,

it's almost funny,

the deluge of money,

barely seen

through the TV screen.

Billions of jabs

a dagger stabs.

Actually, a needle, a syringe,

just the tiniest twinge.

A painless price,

roll the dice.

Healing the sick

with a magic trick.

The BBC plugs

to the suckers and mugs.

A broken land.

Just sleight of hand.

The ease of it.

The cobras spit.

Our COVID split.

Headlines

Hannah Stone

Your parents would curtail conversations with "just got to catch the news" as if current affairs were elusive, or in a hurry to get on. That was before the 'top of the hour' brought iterations of half-fact and supposition, masquerading as stuff we needed to know, to be safe. Predator and victim have exchanged places. When I run from the news, it trips me up, wrapping me in toxic tentacles, stealing my breath. The headlines about the pandemic form their own contagion, can contaminate the whole day if you fail to sanitise your discernment. I try a new approach, breaking time into randomly sized fragments, to minimise exposure to viral load. The top of the hour is humanely decapitated; out stroll favourite epithets, double-entendres and the very best rhetoric. The slack middle of the hour wallows with tripe triplets such as lock, stock and barrel; in no way, shape or form. Depending on the weather, the bottom of the hour is as stinky as slurry, or merely tired and wan. Cliches lacking the will to escape, corny puns and the tautologies of beauticians and influencers slump in damp clumps. If you poke them, they will rouse themselves, and assert their ambition to make it to the top, in bold caps.

Futility

Lee Smith

Two years of misery
But tell me, is it gone
People still are falling ill
I fear it carries on
When they released masses
That was the time to stay at home
Before that I was happy
To be shopping all alone
Masks on, masks off
It drives me round the bend
But I know this bloody COVID
Will get me in the end

A Quick Word From COVID

Rose Stevens

Hello, it's the virus here
I want to make one thing clear
This party's
only just getting started
You say that it's been dragging on
for way too long
it's time to move on
But this isn't how I end
OK people, let's pretend
you ignore your scientist friends
allow rampant transmission
you'll give me permission
to replicate
at such a rate
that in a short time
you'll find I've combined
with other variants of concern
or a different virus, I could turn
more deadly
than I am already
Or maybe I'll acquire a spike
from a virus, whose spike I like
or I'll just keep changing
either way I'll be evading
your vaccines
Do you get what I mean?
Unless you suppress me

things could get messy
You know I'm right
it's there in black and white
in the pages of SAGE's latest report
so maybe give it a little thought
You claim to be the clever ones
while I'm a brainless pathogen
If you lie back and let me win
humans, it's embarrassing

A COVID Christmas

Terri Lee-Shield

Empty buses driving by,
Full moon beaming in the sky.
Twinkle lights in the distance; glisten.
Standing alone in silence listening.

What a year it has been,
The one with the virus.
When we all got locked up,
With no one beside us.

In a world where love is protecting a stranger,
Spending Christmas alone,
And New Year out of danger

Old Lives Matter

Steve Heyes

Younger people ignore instruction,

Hell bent on causing Granny's destruction,

Wild raves in woods causing a ruction,

Police seem unable to properly function,

Society approaching a dangerous junction,

Our future threatened by young with no compunction

Shielders afraid of further lockdown sejunction,

Cases rising daily are witness to the exponential function,

We need to give our young a wise man's gumption,

Before we're all taken by the COVID-19 consumption,

The numbers rise causing worldwide malfunction,

Areas lock down because of social regression,

Driving the economy into a major recession.

A Few Haikus…to Punctuate the Time

Lisa Goodwin

Sat here on my own,
isolation paradox,
I am not alone.

Painfully aware,
this class privilege crisis,
romanticizes.

Dance with disorder,
laughing and baying outside,
the unbelievers.

He thinks I'm deranged,
the man walking past can't see,
my smile through the mask.

Get back to normal?
You must be fucking kidding.
Normal didn't work.

Nature is louder,
outside this quiet stillness,
spring working from home.

A Little Pome for Our Times

Jane Badrock

I caught a little virus, I gave it to my Mum.
She gave it to the neighbours which made the whole street glum.
They all went off to Tesco's to buy some more supplies.
But when they all arrived there, they got a huge surprise.
The food shelves all were empty, the toilet rolls all sold.
Nothing left of use for all the vulnerable and old.
The playground air got cleaner. The seas began to clear.
Environmentalists agreed solutions now were here.
We got a little kinder. We helped, we didn't fuss.
And in return our planet began to care for us.

The Spring of 2020

Andy Cash

In this City we now must wait, watch, walk, want
Millions of us, billions in many countries too
Released to bang and clap once a week for heroes
Welcomed in their tasks of care in human isolation

Forced love, to new friends of old times, in hell
The daily beat, the flogged, the tournament still
Anger inside from human rights and spring scenes
The parklands are where the fight can be lost

Temperatures rise, throats infected, rainbows drawn
The hope, from a bloody-minded man, with medals
His toil, head hunched, smart suit, frame pushed on
A child draws her card for him, never to be forgotten now

The Monarch caged in a castle with her wildly Prince
Celebrities still dance in virtual space whilst others die
Children play, their sounds in the garden, sweeten this day
Brave souls walk on, exhausted, but so relentless

Ways and means to an end game we can talk about
Have we broken our world, or has it just frightened us?
Dawn to dusk, more mouths soon go empty in lockdown mode
The birds still sing, nests are feathered, and life begins.

Ephemeral

Stuart Watkins

Sometimes,
special circumstances make us think.
Ponder the nature of time,
our own mortality,
and our irrelevance and insignificance......

....

What separates a flash, a split-second
from a century?

Content, and context.

What separates the life of a woman, or man
that achieves a million things,
or one monumental thing,
from one that achieves nothing
that anyone remembers?

Content, and context.

What separates those that have lived lives
full of love and happiness
from those that have endured
unfathomable pain and suffering,
and never known a single moment of bliss?

Much, much more than just content and context.
Everything, the world.

Yet in the 'scheme of things'
all lives and all experiences
have a beginning, an end,
and an in-between,
and are gone
as if they never were.

**(From the 2021 abstract collection 'Cosmic Visions.' also as
spoken word on the 2022 song
'Babel' by Dutch band Lesoir.)**

The White Queen

Anna Maria Mickiewicz

White billowing clouds
White lilies of the valley
and white juicy lilies

White fragrant lilacs
White petals on the pavement
White masks on the faces

White English spring
breathes white fog

Lent in a Time of Coronavirus
'The Wet Market Sources of COVID-19: Bats and Pangolins have an Alibi'

Sharon Larkin

A forty-day diet can focus the mind
flatten the curves and trim the behind.
So, in choosing food for a modest dinner
to boost the spirit and make tums thinner,
why not just opt for tomato soup
and leave the bats to dive and swoop?

It would be best to eliminate snacks
to fit back into our jeans and slacks
but if the munchies come upon us
and we're sick of all that hummus,
for our elevenses or for our tiffin,
let's not p-p-pick up a pangolin.

Do you want to stay asymptomatic
of a nasty virus and global pandemic?
Well, here's some advice, long overdue,
when making casserole, hotpot or stew,
a couple of hints and easy quick wins -
just leave out the bats and the pangolins

Taming the flesh refines the spirit,
in time for lots of Easter Eggs, innit?
So as we discipline mind and body,
to purge the flesh of all our gluttony
and deliver ourselves from beastly sins,
let's set free the bats and the pangolins.

**(Previously published online at 'Spilling Cocoa
Over Martin Amis' on 9 April 2022)**

Infected

Lee Smith

It started with a cough
A dry and tingly throat
Within hours a temperature
He was as hot as toast
His breathing became laboured
We put him in his bed
They took him to the hospital
And now my man is dead
They wouldn't let me see him
I buried him alone
This cursed COVID-19
Has left me on my own
I don't know how I'll manage
I have no money coming in
I have a freezer full of food
And 2 bottles of gin
So I'll cook up a good meal
And toast my fellow's life
For now I am a widow
No longer a wife

Birthday and COVID

Janet Tai

Just heard….
COVID data
Rose to
10,000 cases
Per day;

The spike….
Comes from
The Lunar
Festive Season;

People gathering
In droves….
At public places
For…,
It's the seasonal
holidays;

'Tis not….
Surprising
For the spike…,
As most do not
Adhere to
Safety protocol;

And then….
There's me
Poor poor me
I'm ruined;

My promised
Birthday dinner
Is as good as burnt;

Staying home
Is no longer
An option
Boo hoo;

Oh well
Better be safe
Than sorry!

So….
Will someone
Please….
Bring out the
Bucket!!!

A Cosmic COVID-19 Vision

Stuart Watkins

2020.

Clouds of death.
Rivers of death.
Fields of death.
Mountains of death.
Deserts of death.
Seas of death.
Streets of death.

Also, almost unimaginable magnitudes
of money changing hands.

Also, almost unfathomable duplicity,
for personal financial gain,
in the face of global human suffering.
A veritable candy shop
for sweet-toothed entrepreneurs,
corporations, companies -
especially if they have the 'Right' friends.

Have there ever been such raw and ruthless
opportunities in our lifetimes, or ever?

The **masks** and disguises
of the commercial and political operations
fall away, to transparency, on this one,
as do the profits behind the prophets.

The reminders and remainders
of networks of unearned, assumed,
secretive privilege.
Of murky, misplaced, masculine,
Masonic self-importance.
Many people have more intellect
in a Teeny-Tweeny-Tiny-Toe
than in the mind of a pretender,
a make-believe Old Etonian Walter Mitty,
or perhaps a prissy, priapic Prima Donna,
Hand On Cock,
crying, like the proverbial crocodile,
in front of a colostomic camera.

We have been united in, and by, our humanity,
for the most part.
Certainly both the very best and very worst
of human characteristics
have been on wide-open display.

It has been both pathetic and hilarious
in equal measure,
when the effect, backlash,
was the opposite of the intention, which was deceit.

Incompetence, apathy, greed,
self-interest, cronyism,
and swimming-out-of-depth
have been commonplace and routine
in high office.
Unfortunately, but usually.

Normally, to achieve promotions, and seniority,
you have to show that you're good at something.

But this is a brave new world.

There is no need for skills, or knowledge, or competence,
only the right phone numbers on speed-dial.

....

Our world-beating government team
is worthy of Alf Ramsay and Bobby Moore's
conquerors of 1966, and no mistake.
They ooze professionalism, pride,
integrity and honesty, (I'm kidding of course), in fact
ugly nationalism, greed and corruption.
These things have an unmistakable and odious odour.

Yet, simultaneously,
authentic heroes and heroines
battled and fought for others.
Friends and family.
Complete strangers.
Putting their own lives
at the lowest priority.
Not at forbidden piss-ups full of selfish liars.

We've been together through
extreme highs and lows,
seeing sporadic jubilation,
but also, sadly,
widespread grief
and personal pain and calamity.
Our eyes startled, shocked,
exhausted, overwhelmed.

....

The social media platforms.

Their precious, populist pretence
of the power of participation,
and their deafening white noise
of trivial, transitory traffic,
and their smokescreens
of deviousness and deception,
and their unaccountable autonomy,
and their narratives
of negativity, nihilism and nothingness,
consume and cover
the addicted, asphyxiated,
anxiety-drenched, apoplectic
user population
with invisibility cloaks,
worthy of any
wizard, warlock or witch.

They are only,
just like your friendly, trusted,
printed and broadcast media:

Factories of Distraction.
Engines of Illusion.
Creators of Confusion.
Dungeons of Delusion.
Mines and machines
of marauding, manipulative misinformation.
Labyrinths of Lies.

Tabloids full of
taxidermic, totalitarian, trashy,
organised, obtuse and
obstructive opinions.

Facts are in intentionally, deliberately
short supply,
conspicuous by their absence.

As an analogy;
the apparent, amiable assistance
and protection of the fireproof asbestos,
is rapidly replaced and substituted
with crippling, creeping and crushing suffocation
by its invading, insidious fibres and splinters.

Once upon a time,
we were each
a zealous, zestful zygote,
in oceans of oestrogen
and prototypal progesterone,
topographic tales of testosterone,
a lascivious and lecherous lottery
of gregarious and gangrenous
gender games and gambles.
A chromosome cocktail.

So, I spew my spidery spleen
and my sparse, spellbound,
spluttering spirit into space,
through a dreary, deep, dark prism
of desolate, destructive, deathly doorways.

A terrifying triptych -
temptingly tessellated, though torn
by the clustered claret claws
and twisted talons of time's tornado.

The soup of micro-organisms in the sacred Ganges,
the putrid, pyrrhic, purifying flames of the Pyres of Varanasi
and the ever-eternal and immortal venom of Set,
course through our bodies
as cleansing energies,
and illuminate our celestial pathways.

....

In the grotto of occult wisdom sits the Astroscope.

It rests among the mighty, majestic, magnificent,
magickal, mystical, masterful, mythical, marvellous,
mysterious, metaphysical, massive
branches and boughs
of the World Tree,
the legendary Yggdrasil.

These are my Cosmic Visions.
The Coy, Vain, Critical Veins of
my Cold, Vacant Curriculum Vitae,
in the age of the Callous, Vengeful
Corona Virus.

**(From the 2021 abstract poetry collection
'Cosmic Visions')**

Box Car Riding

Steve Heyes

Hobos riding the box car

away from the town

Memories are a scar

That make you buckle down

Other hobos keep their space

All wearing face coverings

To stop them being a test case

Populations indoors cowering

Passing through deserted places

COVID lockdown in full control

Info going into databases

Recording every dead soul

Misguided people's objections

Anger at the mask wearers

Calling for no more restrictions

Believing they are scaremongers

President tells us don't worry

COVID-19 will just go away

It's the false news that's gory

His mentality causes dismay

Holding Republican rallies

None wearing masks

Endangering their grannies

Putting them in an early casket.

An election's coming so they say

But Trump says if he loses

No matter what, he'll stay

Continuing to strike insane poses.

Is he intent on killing them all?

In pursuit of restarting the economy

While he ignores the population fall

Is he guilty of this atrocity?

Perhaps those box car Hobos

Will survive Donald the Virus

While the Capitol Hill toffs

Meet the same end as Cyrus the Virus

Dawn Chorus, May 2020

Sharon Larkin

Today we have the choice
to listen to the doom on the news
and brood about the gloom
of the world we're prisoners in
or we can choose to use
this hour we've been allowed,
before the joggers are about
to overtake us on the path
with their puff-pant breath
trailing in their wake,
before the lycra-ed cyclists
flash their fashion far too close.
We sneak into the pre-dawn light,
while neighbours are still abed.
A benevolent moon
beams down on us,
our satellite, our sputnik
our fellow traveller.
We consider the birds of the air
hear them sing their songs
of cheerful ignorance
of human pestilence and fear,
free to stake their boundaries,
coax mates of matching feather,
or simply state their joy
at nests, full of eggs,
joy at the planet they inhabit.

(Previously published in Black Noire Review, May 2022)

New World Disorder (Chapters 1 - 4)

Hahona Pita Batt
(The Square Peg Scribe Warrior)

Chapter 1

Hydras matriculate in laboratory moist markets
The Earth tilts in pandemic jolted axis
Life ebbs in rot and viral refrain
Omens play out in Nostradamus alchemy
Screaming voices split down the drain in viral mass-turbation
Atmosphere roars in ear raid aerosol spray
Children starve while fat cats count lives.

A new world locked down in calibrated disorder
Pencil plaid players choked in masked charade
Razor wired stockade in totalitarian decree
Passport marginalisation in sheeple propaganda fodder
Dystopian panacea not so far-fetched.

Gestapo police state in truncheon sanctioned inseminate
Geppetto puppetry in pied piper sublimation
Conspiracy theory legs grown in marathon musculature
Prayers offered in penitent proliferate
Hiatus deities out to lunch
Populace voices drown in weaponised rhetoric.

Freedom relegated to page 666 of the dictionary
Abe Lincoln turns in his grave

Bob Marley's three little birds suffocate in lies
Martin Luther King's dream for humanity
evaporates in glass shard tote
Nightmares choked on poisoned straw
Two world wars underpinned freedom
Blood and bone tithes in forgotten annal lore.

Gazillionaires - man game of life consoles
Harlot dirty money turns honest men into whores
And now promises of a great reset
More like bar coded incarceration
Hung drawn and quartered mind genocide
Scrotum squeezed in degenerate subjugate
Green mile traipsers in garotted half-truths.

The God in Heaven has forgotten all our prayers
No more bottles for message pleas
Standing alone for a martyr's cause
Lest not we be forgotten
To stand for humanity
Lest we seal our epitaph burden.

Chapter 2

Medical apartheid in state-sanctioned marginalisation
Subliminal hyperbole in Government decree
Skud missile vitriol in subservient media salvo
Servile sycophants kowtow in broken-backed stoop
Hypodermic populace gifts in death chamber prick
Nuremberg conventions drowned in ether placate
Two world wars now we scourge with domestic foe.

Coercive matriculate in dystopian subjugate
Decapitation of emancipation in needled visage
Unceremoniously crucified in Nazarene noose
Biblical revelations in bar code indoctrinate
Ever decreasing circles in propaganda snare
Principle opposed in belligerent vehemence
Fascist tyrannical state in totalitarian venerate
Free thought genocide in Fuhrer gesticulate
Mass-turbation in smoke and mirror waxed quim
Bonfired human rights in napalm ash
Logan Run omen in dystopian dogma.

Wet market last supper smorgasbord
Epidemiologist pied piper conductors
Naysayer voices silenced by bullshit baffled brains
Peaceful protest in seductive vociferate -
militant constabulary asphyxiate
free speech in road spike ejaculate
Freedom just a notion in dreamstate escape
Binary coded humans in legislative flagellate
Hominid rendered distillate in servile tow
Never forget Tianenmen…
subjugated and relegated…
populace primed for army tank ichored snow.

Chapter 3

Vulcanised totalitarianism
Alligator dosed Dr. Seuss viral spin

Big pharma fiscal degenerates
Naysayer execution in parasitic red tape

Political dribble in jismed digest
Ephemeral citizen coagulate

Tupping harnessed sheeple
Binary bar coded purgatory
Freedom a womb barren echo from the past.
Emancipation fossilised in flaccid wrist ejaculate
Pacified in artificial inseminate
State sanctioned democratic annihilate
Mind cauterise in free choice castrate
Subterfuge servile sycophants
Weep not in vain fickle little minions.
Shear the sheeple putting paid to want
Plug the politicians mouths with despot spoil
Paint their eyes with the lanolin sweat of persecution
Fill their ears with protest echoed voices
Burden their hands with the weight of starvation
Yoke their backs with bereavement tithes of the poor
Open their minds with righteous flagellation
Repay them in kind with pole stripped subliminal indoctrination
De-slime the K-Y Jelly
Vaccine-proof their mandates
Then and only then release them
to the good shepherd's fold.

Chapter 4

Geppetto string the populace in rhetorical oppress
Jugular squeeze 'til the bastards bleed and tap out
Pandora's had a gutful - eloping in prima face shit-faced ado
More rise and fall than a whore's drawers

Pinocchio's poor old nose grows shorter by the day
Shutter the eyes of scientific minds

Sow seeds to inoculate contradiction
Improvise in righteous misquote
and polarising diarrhoea terse.

Wineskin gag grapevine agitators
Propagandise in virulent market moist strain
Ear wet deweaponise teetotaller minds
Pronoun renounce the obdurate informed
Mete out resistance in eunuch emasculate
Ameliorate conspiracies in nuclear half-life bias.

Political inculcate in spin doctor inseminate
Supplicate those of virginal yield
Pare the petals and deflorate the dregs
Brain condition until shampoo comatose
Dehumanise in hospital grade mask
Wash their hands in the Fuhrer's spittoon
Stereotype the victims in psychological defeat
Non compos mentis palette pitch.

Promise fascist salvation to veto terminal judgement
A Garden of Eden in isotope hash
Artifice their minds in fissile reconnaissance
Domicile free will into halfway hell
Bifurcate their aspirations in viral overload

Lipstick kiss the arses of politicians
Sermon mass in baptismal hysteria
Parishioners line streets in kowtow and stoop.

Pandemic

Sarah Laurel

A time when we knew our neighbours
Good deeds and errands were run
Laughing in cobbled streets while
whitewashing doorsteps and
getting jobs done.
Sheets over streets hanging on Mondays.

In years to come we'd have
World Wide Web
Get on your LAN, interconnected by WAN,
Find a man, a fan, be on a ban!

Back in time to '53 when DNA discovery
marked a milestone in history!
2020, a new vaccine paradigm.
Standing on the shoulders of giants,
the race is on
I loved Captain Tom.

Temporality of time!

Lockdown.

What was yours and mine?

Was it an escape, a chance to breathe, or marvel at
what keyworkers achieve?
It's been going on through history,

Pandemic

it's nothing new,
but before,
it didn't affect
ME
&
YOU.

Printed in Great Britain
by Amazon

83780335R10072